Read All About Sharks

SHARKS AND PEOPLE

Lynn Stone

The Rourke Corporation, Inc.
Vero Beach, Florida 32964

PHOTO CREDITS
©Tom Campbell: cover; ©Marty Snyderman: p.4, 6, 9, 16, 22; ©David Fleetham/INNERSPACE VISIONS: p.7; ©Herb Segars: p.10; ©Doug Perrine: p.12, 20; ©Lynn M. Stone: p.13; ©Ron and Valerie Taylor/ INNERSPACE VISIONS: p.15; ©Dr. Samuel H. Gruber/ INNERSPACE VISIONS: p.18; ©Mark Colin/INNERSPACE VISIONS: p.19

Library of Congress Cataloging-in-Publication Data

Stone, Lynn M.
  Sharks and people / by Lynn M. Stone
    p. cm. — (Read all about sharks)
  Includes index.
  Summary: Briefly describes how people fish for sharks, photograph and study them, use them for food or other products, and the dangers humans face from sharks and vice versa.
    ISBN 0-86593-446-0 (alk. paper)
    1. Sharks—Juvenile literature. 2. Human-animal relationships—Juvenile literature. [1. Sharks.]
  I. Title II. Series: Stone, Lynn M. Read all about sharks
  QL638.9.S8485 1996
  597'.31—dc20   96–7969
                                                              CIP
                                                               AC

Printed in the USA

TABLE OF CONTENTS

SHARKS AND PEOPLE

People have feared sharks for hundreds of years. Sharks can be dangerous, but they are not all huge, savage killers.

Most kinds of sharks will not grow anywhere near as long as you are tall. Sharks rarely attack people, but people kill millions of sharks each year.

Not everyone fears or hates sharks. Some people fish just for big sharks. Some divers plunge into the sea just to watch sharks.

Shark divers enjoy seeing wild sharks close-up in the shark's own undersea world.

SHARKS AND SPORT

Many divers photograph sharks. The diver may swim freely, like the shark, or work from inside a steel-barred cage.

Some free-swimming divers tag along with huge whale sharks, 40-foot-long giants that are the biggest fish in the world (see the cover).

A diver photographs a Caribbean reef shark.

Bronze whaler shark approaches divers in a steel cage in South Australia.

People who catch sharks for sport on fishing poles usually work from boats. Certain kinds of sharks, such as shortfin makos, are strong fighters. They make great sport and good eating.

SHARKS FOR FOOD

People use sharks in many ways. Most **species** (SPEE sheez), or kinds, of sharks can be eaten. Shark steaks and fins are sold throughout the world. Shark fins are used to make sharkfin soup.

Two species that fishermen love to catch are among the tastiest sharks. They are the shortfin mako and great white. The porbeagle and piked dogfish are also sharks commonly used for food.

This fisherman's prize is a great white shark, a popular source of food and sport.

SHARK PRODUCTS

Sharkskin is rough, like sandpaper. It can be treated, however, and made into soft, smooth leather.

Sharkskin leather is used for boots, purses, belts, and wallets. Shark jaws are sold for wall hangings. Shark teeth are used in jewelry.

Shark livers provide huge amounts of oil. The oil used to be a valuable source of vitamin A. Today vitamin A can be made in laboratories, and oil itself is found elsewhere.

This small mako shark could have its jaw turned into a wall hanging, its flesh into food, and its skin into leather.

STUDY OF SHARKS

Scientists study sharks to learn more about them and how they might be of more use to people. Scientists tag sharks to find out how long they live, how fast they grow, and where they go.

A University of Hawaii scientist tags a big tiger shark so that the animal's movements can be studied.

At Mote Laboratory in Florida, scientists study sharks. Visitors can watch sharks and other fish at the lab's indoor-outdoor aquarium.

Sharks seem to be free of diseases and lumps called **tumors** (TOO merz). Scientists would like to know why. The answers might help people deal with human diseases.

Sharks are difficult to study in the ocean. Many shark studies take place in marine labs, places where ocean creatures are the subjects.

SHARK ATTACKS

Scientists also want to know more about why sharks sometimes attack for no clear reason.

Sharks do not attack people often. In the United States, someone's chance of drowning in the sea is 1,000 times greater than dying of shark bites. When a shark does attack, it usually bites, then swims away. About one person in four who is bitten by a shark dies.

Studies by Mote Marine Laboratory in Florida showed that shark attacks often took place in water less than five feet deep.

Australian spear fisherman Rodney Fox shows three-week-old scars from an attack by a great white shark.

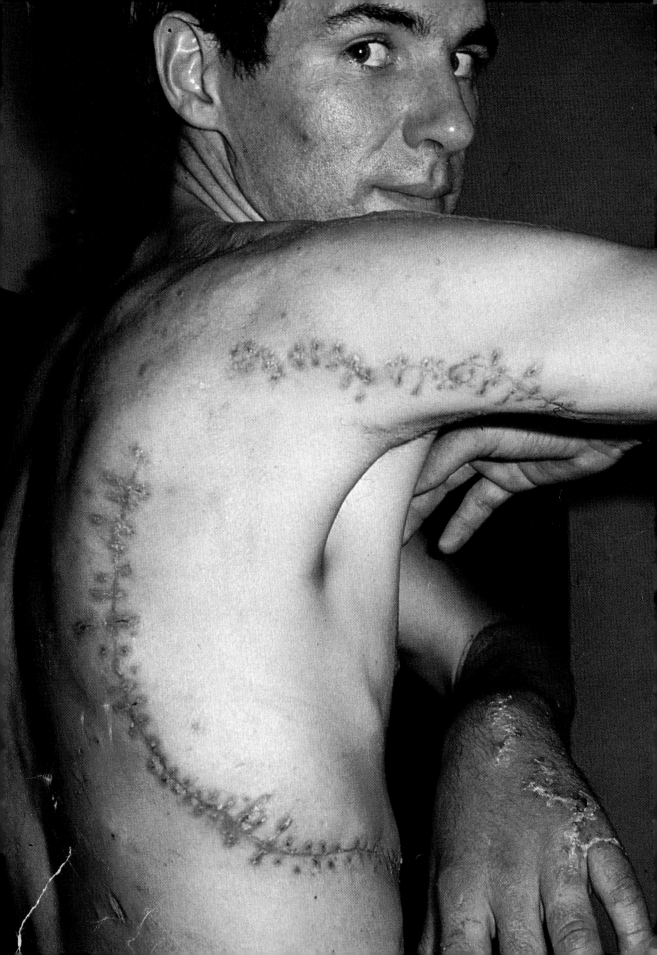

SAFETY WITH SHARKS

You can reduce even the unlikely chance of shark attack. Don't swim alone or at beaches where sharks are commonly seen.

Never swim in the sea at night or along beaches where people are fishing. Injured fish attract larger fish.

Don't swim where there are sudden changes from shallow water to deep. If you see small fish rushing towards shore or skipping across the ocean surface, leave the water.

Don't wear flashy objects, like jewelry, into the sea.

A diver handles a silky shark to remove an old fish hook. Divers reduce chances of shark attack by diving in pairs or groups.

SHARKS IN TROUBLE

Each year shark attacks kill fewer than 100 people throughout the world. On the other hand, people kill more than 100 million sharks each year.

With so many sharks being speared, hooked, and netted, some species are in trouble. They are disappearing faster than they can replace themselves.

Shark carcasses were wasted after a sport fishing tournament in Montauk, New York.

Shark fins dry for the market in Baja California.

Millions of sharks are used for dog food. Thousands more are caught in gill nets, where they drown and rot.

SAVING SHARKS

Sharks have been overfished partly because they have been so feared and hated. Now scientists caution that the ocean world needs sharks. The ocean's health depends upon a healthy balance. It needs larger **predators**, (PRED uh terz) like sharks, to keep the number of smaller creatures under control.

Some nations and states are coming to the shark's rescue. Gill netting is now against the law in most places. Huge ocean **reserves** (re ZERVZ) are being set aside where all marine animals are protected.

Fear of big, toothy sharks like this tiger shark caught off Florida has led to overkill of sharks.

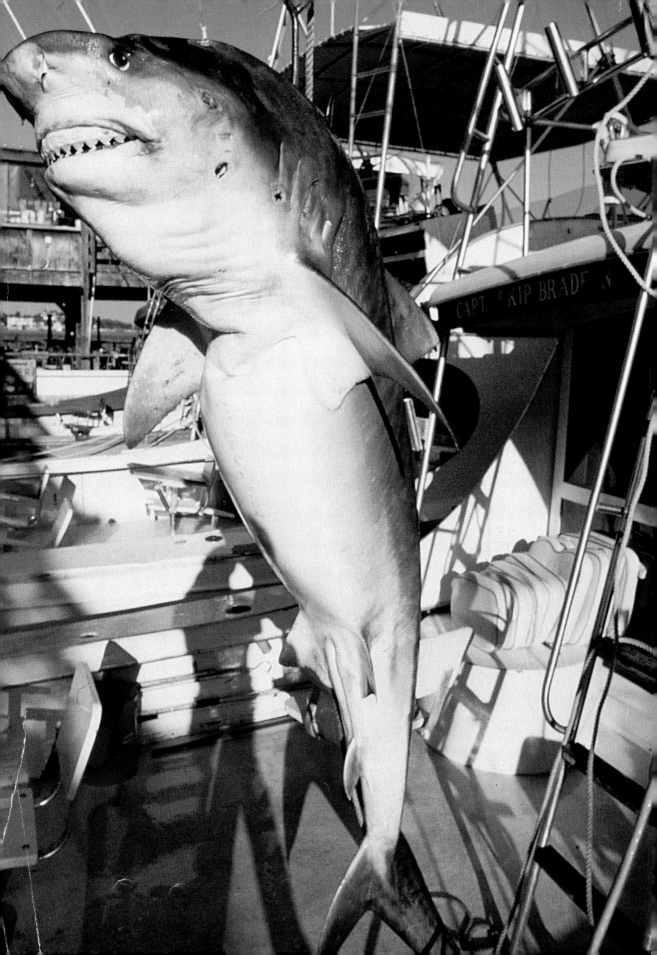

GLOSSARY

marine (muh REEN) — of or relating to the ocean

predators (PRED uh terz) — animals that hunt other animals for food

reserves (re ZERVZ) — areas set aside for the protection of animals and plants

species (SPEE sheez) — within a group of closely related animals, one certain kind, such as a *great white* shark.

tumors (TOO merz) — abnormal lumps of body tissue that arise and grow for no apparent reason

More people are beginning to understand the need for a healthy shark population in the ocean world.

INDEX